World About Us

Coal

By Kate Bedford

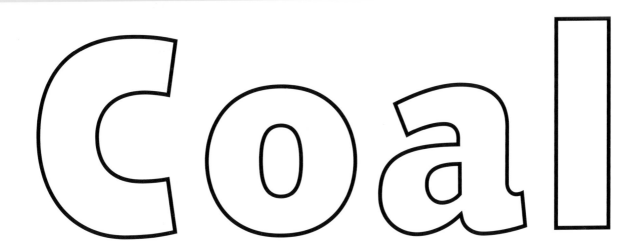

Stargazer Books

Designed and produced by
Aladdin Books Ltd

First published in the
United States in 2007 by
Stargazer Books
c/o The Creative Company
123 South Broad Street
P.O. Box 227
Mankato, Minnesota 56002

Printed in the United States

Editor:
Harriet Brown

Designer:
Flick, Book Design and Graphics

Illustrations:
Ian Thompson

Picture researcher:
Alexa Brown

Consultants:
Jackie Holderness—former Senior
Lecturer in Primary Education,
Westminster Institute,
Oxford Brookes University

Rob Bowden—education consultant,
author, and photographer specializing
in social and environmental issues.

Library of Congress Cataloging-
in-Publication Data

Bedford, Kate.
  Energy : coal / by Kate Bedford.
  p. cm. -- (World about us)
  ISBN- 978-1-59604-109-7
  1. Power resources--Juvenile literature. 2.
Coal--Juvenile literature. I. Title. II. World
about us (North Mankato, Minn.).

TJ163.23.B43 2006
333.793'2--dc22

2005056745

CONTENTS

Notes to parents and teachers

This series has been developed for group use in the classroom, as well as for children reading alone. In particular, its text on two levels allows children of mixed abilities to enjoy reading about the same topic. The larger size text (A, below) offers apprentice readers a simplified text. This simplified text is used in the introduction to each chapter and in the picture captions. This font is part of the © Sassoon family of fonts whose maximum legibility is recommended for early readers. The smaller size text (B, below) offers a more challenging read for older or more able readers.

Coal mining today

**Coal is mined,
both underground
and near the surface.**

 **Strip mining is done
on or near the surface.**

These mines have coal seams
within 600 feet (200m)
of the surface.

A

B

Questions, key words, and glossary

Each spread ends with a question that parents and teachers can use to discuss and develop further ideas and concepts. Further questions are provided in a quiz on page 30. A reduced version of pages 30 and 31 is shown below. The illustrated "Key words" section is provided as a revision tool, particularly for apprentice readers, in order to help with spelling, writing, and guided reading. The glossary is for more able or older readers.

In addition to the glossary's role as a reference aid, it is also designed to reinforce new vocabulary and provide a tool for further discussion and revision. When glossary terms first appear in the text, they are highlighted in bold.

 See how much you know!

How many types of coal are there?

What is coal made from?

What is strip mining?

Which types of transportation was coal used to power in the past?

How is coal transported today?

Coal is used in the making of which metal?

Can you name some things that are made from coal?

Why does burning coal cause problems?

How can we help to save coal?

Key words

Miner

A

Fuel

Energy   **Fossil fuel**

Gas   **Geologist**

Pollution   **Steel**

Seam

Glossary

Acid rain—Gases released by burning fuels enter the atmosphere. They mix with water and fall to the ground as acid rain.

Blast furnace—A very hot oven in which the metal iron is melted out of iron ore.

Coal reserves—Coal that is still in the ground that we can mine and use in the future.

Global warming—An increase in the temperature on Earth. This may be caused by a buildup of carbon dioxide and other gases in the atmosphere.

B

Recycle—To reuse waste material and make it into something new.

Renewable energy—Sources of energy that, unlike fossil fuels, will never run out, e.g. wind, water, and solar energy.

Turbine—An engine that spins and generates electricity.

What is coal?

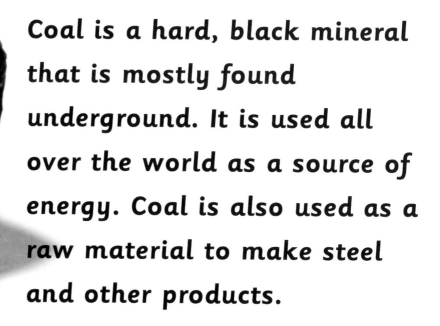

Coal is a hard, black mineral that is mostly found underground. It is used all over the world as a source of energy. Coal is also used as a raw material to make steel and other products.

▶ **Burning coal gives off a lot of heat.**

Coal is used as a fuel because it burns so well. A lump of coal burns slowly on the outside and gives off heat for a long time. Coal contains a substance called carbon and this is the part of coal that burns. After coal has burned, all that is left is a gray dust called ash.

There are three different types of coal.

Coal varies in hardness, color, and the amount of heat it releases when it burns. The three types of coal are not found in the same mine.

1. Lignite—Lignite coal is dry and crumbly. It contains about 50 percent carbon. It burns slowly with a yellow, smoky flame, and gives off the least heat and the most pollution.

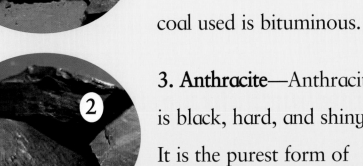

2. Bituminous coal—Bituminous coal is fairly hard. It has a sheen and a layered texture. Bituminous coal contains more carbon than lignite but

less than anthracite. It burns well and makes a little smoke. Most of the coal used is bituminous.

3. Anthracite—Anthracite is black, hard, and shiny. It is the purest form of coal and is 90 percent carbon. Anthracite contains the most energy, burns hottest, gives off the most heat, and makes hardly any smoke. It is the best coal for heating and cooking.

How are most houses heated today?

How is coal formed?

Coal is a fossil fuel like oil and gas. It is made from the remains of ancient plants. Over millions of years the plants have changed into coal. Some coal was formed even before dinosaurs roamed the earth.

▲ ▶ Coal is made from the plants that grew in swampy forests.

Most coal used today was formed during the Carboniferous Period (which means "age of the coal forests.") This period happened 360-286 million years ago, when the earth's climate was warm, wet, and humid. Younger lignite coals were formed much later, in the Cretaceous Period, 144-65 million years ago, and in the Tertiary Period, 65-2 million years ago.

Coal forms underground very slowly.

1. Plants die and fall to the bottom of swamps, forming a thick layer of rotting plant material called peat.

2. The plant remains become buried by layers of mud and silt.

4. Over millions of years, the plants change into coal through a process called coalification. Pressure, heat, time, and chemical processes gradually

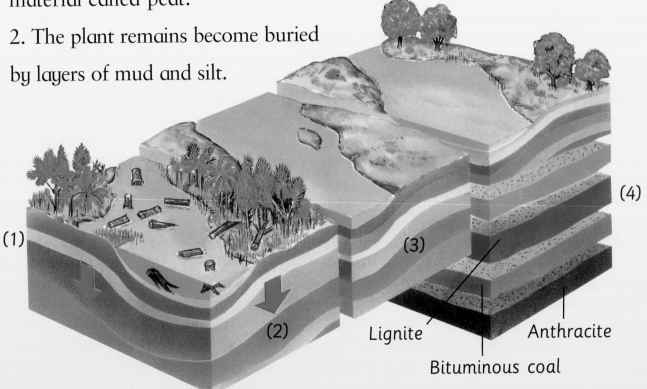

(1)

(2)

(3)

(4)

Lignite

Bituminous coal

Anthracite

3. As the plant remains are buried deeper, they become more squashed and heated.

change the dead plants into mineral form. First they change into lignite, then bituminous coal, and finally become anthracite.

 Why is coal called a fossil fuel?

Coal in the past

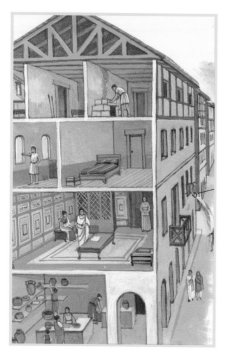

People have been using coal for thousands of years. The Chinese were probably the first to use coal. They burned it as a fuel more than three thousand years ago. Other people, such as Hopi Indians of North America and the Ancient Greeks and Romans (left), also used coal.

► **Coal was used to power the first factories.**

Beginning in the mid-18th century, the demand for coal grew and grew as more factories were built. This was a time known as the Industrial Revolution. Coal was needed to power the steam engines that ran the machines in factories. Many large towns sprang up with hundreds of smoking chimneys.

◀ Coal is burned in steam engines in trains.

Around 100 years ago, most trains and ships were powered by steam engines. A coal fire was used to heat tanks of water to produce steam. The steam was used to push and pull pistons that made the train's wheels turn. On steam ships, the pistons turned the propeller.

Coal gas, made from coal, was used to light street lamps.

In the early 1800s, coal gas was produced by burning coal. Originally, coal gas was burned in street lamps. Each evening, lamplighters would light the lamps and return again the following morning to turn them off. Later, coal gas was used for cooking and heating. It was replaced by natural gas in the 1960s.

 Why do you think coal gas was used to light street lamps?

Finding coal

Coal is found in layers in the ground called seams. Coal seams can be bent or shifted by movements in the earth's crust. Some coal seams have risen right up to the earth's surface. Other coal seams are found buried deep underground.

► **Geologists explode rocks to help them find coal.**

Geologists, people who study rocks, look for clues that show where coal might be in the ground. They survey and study an area, and may decide to set off explosions in the ground. The geologists measure the speed that the explosion's shock waves travel through the rock. This helps them to make maps of the underground rocks that may contain coal.

◀ Holes are drilled into the ground. Rock samples are removed.

If geologists find an area where there might be coal, they do more tests. A drilling rig removes rods of rock from under the ground. These rock samples are examined for coal. If enough good quality coal is found, it will be worth sinking a mine.

Coal is found all over the world.

Coal is found on every continent and in over 70 countries. China is the biggest producer of coal in the world. There are an estimated one trillion tons (909 billion tonnes) of proven **coal reserves** worldwide. The biggest coal reserves are in the U.S., Russia, China, and India.

This map shows where coal reserves are found in billions of tons / metric tons:

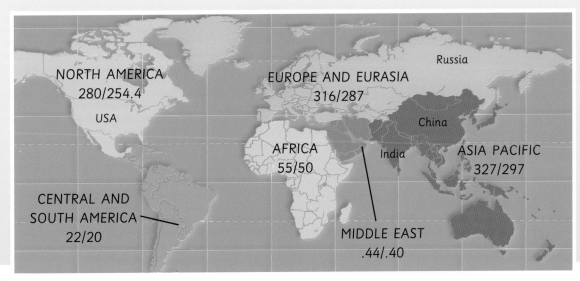

NORTH AMERICA
280/254.4

USA

EUROPE AND EURASIA
316/287

Russia

China

AFRICA
55/50

India

ASIA PACIFIC
327/297

CENTRAL AND
SOUTH AMERICA
22/20

MIDDLE EAST
.44/.40

 Why do people only mine for coal where the coal seams are big?

Coal mining today

Coal is mined both underground and near the surface. Machines work deep underground to drill the coal. It is then taken to the surface by elevators. Giant diggers are used to mine the surface coal.

 Strip mining is done on or near the surface.

These mines have coal seams within 600 feet (200m) of the surface. The top layer of soil is scraped away. Any rocks are broken up using explosives and are then removed. The coal underneath is mined by giant diggers and excavators. Strip mining sites are huge and can cover many square miles.

Mines go deep underground.

Coal is mined by digging a mine shaft down to reach the coal seams. Miners use machinery such as automatic drills and cutters to dig out the coal along the seam. Coal is carried on conveyor belts to the mine shaft where it is put into containers and taken to the surface.

Coal mining is a very dirty job.

Miners work underground in hot conditions, with black coal dust everywhere. Breathing in coal dust can clog the miners' lungs and cause diseases. Mining can also be dangerous. When underground, miners must wear a protective hard hat with a light on it in case the electric lighting system fails. There is always the possibility of collapsing shafts, together with pockets of dangerous gases.

 Why is coal mining a dangerous job?

Transporting coal

Coal needs to be transported from the coal mine to wherever it is used. Coal is heavy and bulky to carry. Transporting it by road or by air would cost too much. So coal is carried by ships and trains, which are slower but cheaper.

 Coal is carried along rivers and across oceans.

Coal is transported along rivers by barges. Rivers like the Rhine in Germany are full of barges carrying coal inland. Coal is transported around the world by sea. For example, ships carry coal mined in Australia thousands of miles to countries in Southeast Asia and Europe.

Coal trains can be 100 freight cars long.

Coal trains carry coal long distances from the mines. They travel at a slow, steady pace because the coal is so heavy. Each car on the train can carry up to 100 tons of coal. One carload of coal has enough fuel to last just 20 minutes at a coal-fired power plant.

Coal is sorted by size and cleaned, ready for use.

Coal preparation plants wash the coal with water which removes dirt, rocks, and some of the chemical sulfur. Preparing the coal helps to remove harmful substances that can cause pollution when the coal is used. This makes the coal burn more efficiently and reduces the air pollution.

 If a freight car carries 100 tons of coal, how many tons can a 100-car train carry?

Using coal today

Coal is used as a source of energy. Over half the world's coal is burned to make electricity. Coal produces 39 percent of the world's electricity. It is also used to make heat energy for industry. Coal is burned in ovens, forges, and kilns.

► **Coal is burned in power plants to make electricity.**

Before coal is used this way, it is crushed into a powder to make it burn better and hotter. When the coal burns at a high temperature it heats water in a boiler to produce steam. The steam spins **turbines** that drive generators which produce electricity. The electricity is sent along cables to homes and businesses.

Coal energy is used for many things, including the making of cement.

The main uses of coal are as follows:

Electricity generation	62%
Steelmaking	16%
Transport and other industry	10%
Cement	5%
Domestic	5%
Other uses	2%

Coal can be made into a liquid fuel.

Coal can be converted into a liquid fuel in a process called liquification. Liquid coal can be refined (made purer) and used instead of crude oil. It can be made into a fuel for transportation. One third of South Africa's liquid fuel is made from coal.

 What else can be burned in power plants to make electricity?

Coal products

Apart from liquid fuel (see pg 19), coal can be made into many different products. These include coke, used for steelmaking, soap, and pitch. A sticky, black substance, pitch is used to waterproof roofs.

▶ **Coal is used to make steel from iron.**

Bituminous coal is heated to 2,192°F (1,200°C) without air, which turns it into a substance called coke. Coke and rock containing iron are heated in a **blast furnace**. Coke burns at a higher temperature than coal and separates the iron from the rock, making molten iron ore. The molten ore is then mixed with carbon to make steel.

This soap is made from coal.

When bituminous coal is heated to make coke, it gives off gases. These gases are collected and cooled into a liquid called coal tar. Coal tar is a black, oily liquid that is used to make soap and ointments for skin conditions such as eczema.

Other coal products include creosote and activated carbon.

Creosote is a black liquid made from coal tar. It is painted onto wooden fences and buildings because it helps stop wood from rotting. Activated carbon from coal is used in water filters and in some hospital machines.

 Can you name some things that are made from steel?

Coal and pollution

Mining coal can leave mounds of waste (known as slag) on the surface, or large scars on the land. Burning coal can cause pollution that can poison plants and wildlife. Today, much effort is put into reducing the pollution from coal (see pages 24-25).

◀ **Mining coal spoils the countryside.**

Coal mines produce mountainous piles of waste slag that can be dangerous and slippery. In 1966, a slag heap collapsed and slid down onto a school in Wales, killing 144 people. Strip mining can leave gaping holes in the land that ruin the landscape. This mining also creates a lot of dust and noise, and can cause water pollution.

▶ Burning coal can cause damage to buildings and trees.

Gases are released from the chimneys of coal-fired power plants and factories. The gases mix with water in the clouds and help to cause **acid rain**. Over time, acid rain can kill plants and wildlife, damage buildings, and pollute rivers and lakes. Winds can carry acid rain thousands of miles.

Burning coal and other fuels gives off damaging gases.

Levels of carbon dioxide in the air are rising as more fossil fuels, including coal, are burned. Industry in China and other Asian countries is growing fast. After the U.S., China is the largest producer of the world's carbon dioxide emissions. Carbon dioxide and other gases trap heat around the earth, making it warm up. This process is known as **global warming**.

 What problems will global warming cause?

Cleaner coal

Using coal now is cleaner than it was in the past. Scientists have found better ways to burn coal so that it does not produce as much pollution. More care is being taken to repair the damage caused by mining.

▶ This man is planting young trees in an old strip mining site.

Strip mining is only a temporary use of the land. When the mining stops, the land can be reclaimed. The land is reshaped and soil is replaced and reseeded. Trees are planted and animals are reintroduced. Reclaimed land can be used for farming, forestry, or wildlife reserves, or flooded to make a lake. Some disused mines are made into landfill sites for garbage disposal.

New power plants are much cleaner.

Modern coal-fired power plants produce more electricity, less carbon dioxide, and fewer harmful chemicals. They are up to 50 percent more efficient than older power plants built in the 1950s. Older, less efficient power plants are being shut down in some countries. China is building power plants that use new technologies to generate more electricity and produce less pollution.

▲ **The gases are cleaned before they leave this chimney.**

Pollution from power plants has been reduced by cleaning the waste gases. Small pieces of soot, harmful gases, and metals are removed. Electric air filters remove dust and small particles. Fabric filters collect particles by sieving, and limestone scrubbers take out harmful gases.

 How long might it take to restore a strip mining site to nature?

Coal for the future

New ways to get energy from coal are being invented. These include making gas from coal deep underground. New methods will also be used to stop so much carbon dioxide gas from being released into the air from power plants. This will help to reduce pollution.

▶ **Carbon dioxide may be stored in empty oil or gas fields underground.**

A new method called Carbon Capture and Storage is being researched. It will catch and remove carbon dioxide from the waste gases produced by coal-fired power plants. When other fuels, such as oil and gas, have been taken out of the ground (1), the space that is left could be filled with waste carbon dioxide from power plants (2).

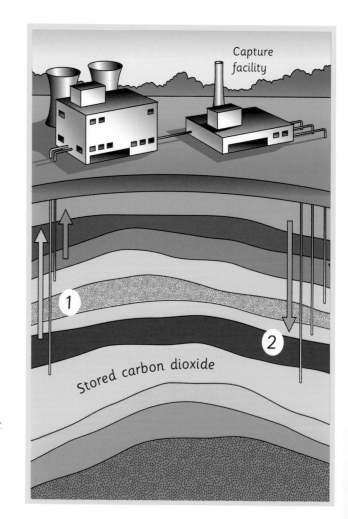

Capture facility

Stored carbon dioxide

1

2

► Coal deep underground is made into gas at this factory.

Rather than bringing coal to the surface, this plant converts coal into gas deep underground. The gas is treated to remove carbon dioxide, and is then used for industrial heating, to generate electricity, or to make into chemicals. Burning this gas releases very little carbon dioxide into the air.

Electricity can be made more cleanly without coal.

Dams, wind turbines, and solar panels generate electricity from water, wind, and the sun without creating pollution. Unlike coal, these are **renewable energy** sources—they will not run out. At present, they only provide a tiny fraction of energy production, but one day they will help us rely less on coal.

 How can solar panels help to reduce global warming?

Saving energy

Scientists think there is enough available coal to last us about 200 years. One day coal will run out. If we use less coal, it will last longer. There are many things we can do to help use less energy and save coal.

▶ **Recycling saves energy.**

Recycling empty bottles and cans can help save coal. Making new steel from used steel uses just a quarter of the energy needed to make it from raw materials. Every ton of recycled steel cans saves half a ton of coke (see pg 20). Recycling aluminum cans saves even more energy. It uses just five percent of the energy needed to make new aluminum from its raw materials.

Why not try some of these ways to save coal?

By using less electricity you can save coal. Take these simple steps and use less electricity.

Turn off lights when you leave the room.

Do not leave the television on standby—it uses up to 60 percent of its switched-on energy.

Use low-energy light bulbs. Each bulb only uses a quarter of the electricity used by an ordinary bulb.

Do not fill a kettle up every time you boil it. Only boil the amount of water you need.

If you can, hang your laundry outside to dry instead of putting it in the dryer.

 How could you and your family save coal?

How many types of coal are there?

What is coal made from?

What is strip mining?

Which types of transportation was coal used to power in the past?

How is coal transported today?

Coal is used in the making of which metal?

Can you name some things that are made from coal?

Why does burning coal cause problems?

How can we help to save coal?

Key words

Miner

Fuel	**Electricity**
Energy	**Fossil fuel**
Gas	**Geologist**
Pollution	**Steel**

Seam

Glossary

Acid rain—Gases released by burning fuels enter the atmosphere. They mix with water and fall to the ground as acid rain.

Blast furnace—A very hot oven in which the metal iron is melted out of iron ore.

Coal reserves—Coal that is still in the ground that we can mine and use in the future.

Global warming—An increase in the temperature on Earth. This may be caused by a buildup of carbon dioxide and other gases in the atmosphere.

Recycle—To reuse waste material and make it into something new.

Renewable energy—Sources of energy that, unlike fossil fuels, will never run out, e.g. wind, water, and solar energy.

Turbine—An engine that spins. A turbine uses water, wind, or steam power to spin and generate electricity.

Index

Photocredits:
Abbreviations: l-left, r-right, b-bottom, t-top, c-center, m-middle. Front cover – Flat Earth. Back cover – Digital Vision. 5br, 12br, 31bl – Chuck Meyers, Office of Surface Mining, 3tl, 11tl, 24tl – Corbis, 11br, 29ml – Corel, 20br – Corus, 27tl – © David Price Photography, 3tml, 15mr – Dermot Tatlow/Panos Pictures, 2-3 – Flat Earth, 12tl – John Howell, University of Bergen, 13tl – Photo by Ted Nield © The Geological Society of London, www.geolsoc.org.uk, 24br, 25tl, 26br, 28tl – Photodisc, 26tl, 27mr – Select Pictures, 5tl, 7t, 7m, 7b, 30tr – University of Wisconsin-Milwaukee Geography Department, 1, 3bml, 3bl, 5bl, 5tr, 14tl, 15tr, 17bl, 19bl, 25br, 29tr, 29bl, 30br, 31tl – US Department of Energy, 4ml, 4bl, 5ml, 6tl, 6br, 8tl, 10br, 14ml, 16tl, 16ml, 17tr, 18tl, 18br, 19tr, 20tr, 21tr, 21bl, 22tr, 22bl, 23bl, 23tr, 27bl, 27br, 30mr – www.istockphoto.com